the easy way to walk in the spirit

hearing God's voice and following His direction

by
larry huggins,
Ambassador of Christ

Harrison House
Tulsa, Oklahoma

09 08 07 06 05   10 9 8 7 6 5 4 3 2 1

The Easy Way To Walk in the Spirit:
Hearing God's Voice and Following His Direction
ISBN 1-57794-529-8
Copyright © 2005 by Larry Huggins
P.O. Box 140645
Austin, TX 78714
1-888-YES-LIFE

Published by Harrison House, Inc.
P.O. Box 35035
Tulsa, Oklahoma 74153

dedication

To my friends and mentors, John and Pat Avanzini. Thank you for blazing a wide trail for Loretta and me to follow. You've made our journey easier.

contents

introduction

Think how different your lifestyle would be if you knew how to walk in the Spirit. You could be at the right place at the right time, avoid pitfalls, meet the right people, make better decisions. Walking in the Spirit, or being Spirit-led, is possible for all of God's children.

But to some, walking in the Spirit is a mystery. Others make it more complicated than it is. One time a friend said to me, "I know when I'm walking in the Spirit. I get a warm velvety feeling on the inside."

"Ha!" I laughed. "I get that feeling when I eat a hot fudge sundae."

Believe me, there's an easier and more accurate way to be led by the Spirit, and you're going to learn about it in this book. Even if you have experience in being Spirit-led, it will be good for you to read about it again and hone your knowledge. You may learn some things you didn't know.

Walking in the Spirit means having His guidance and assistance in our daily lives—and God expects all of us to walk that way.

"For as many as are led by the Spirit of God, they are the sons of God."

ROMANS 8:14

In many years of international ministry and extensive travel, I've come to depend on the Holy Spirit's guidance.

Once, long before we made Mexico our home, my wife, Loretta, and I were in the capital city of Guanajuato. We wanted to get better acquainted with a pastor who lived in Léon, about forty-five minutes away by bus. The problem was, all we had was his name and the name of his church— no address or phone number—and he lived in a city of more than a million inhabitants (in which very few were born-again believers).

In spite of all that, I said to Loretta, "Let's go in faith; the Holy Spirit will guide us."

We made the trip and soon arrived in Léon, stepped off the bus, and walked over to the taxi zone. There were at least two dozen taxis lined up.

I approached the first taxi and asked the driver, "Do you know of a church called Amistad Cristiana?"

He shook his head no (I had the name wrong). So I walked around for a few moments and prayed in the Spirit.[1] Then, I approached the second cab driver who I noticed was looking at me. I repeated my question, "Do you know of a church called Amistad Cristiana?"

"No, not in Léon," he said emphatically. "In Mexico City, yes, but not here. What's the pastor's name?" I answered, "Filepe Del Castillo."

He said, "He's my pastor, you're Larry Huggins, and the church you're looking for is called Trigo y Miel. We're five minutes away from the church; get in and I'll take you there for free."

Wow! What are the odds of that being a mere coincidence? I can easily give you a thousand exciting examples like that. These kinds of experiences happen to us almost every day because we know how to walk in the Spirit.

hearing from God

In the following pages, I'm going to teach you what I call *The Easy Way To Walk in the Spirit.* Understand that there are many ways to hear from God—dreams, visions, diverse tongues, and the interpretation of diverse tongues[2] among others. God reveals things to us however the Spirit wills. But what I'm going to share with you is what I call the default method of hearing from God. It works all the time—even when the dreams and visions aren't coming.

In life, when we have to make decisions on the fly, what are we going to do? Lie down, take a nap, and hope we receive a dream from God? That won't serve us. God may use dreams and visions in guiding us (if He so desires), but we shouldn't expect Him to only use that method. Dreams and visions may come, but as we will see, we are to operate according to the Word of God.

God tells us in His Word that He wants us to be prosperous (3 John 2) not only to bless us, but to enable us to serve Him in a greater capacity. So who knows, maybe you will become rich or famous because of what you receive from this little book. Well, be sure to remember me when you come into your kingdom!

What you are about to learn will always work, anywhere, anytime—that is, if you take it to heart and apply it right. I know it works because I've worked it for years, ever since the Holy Spirit revealed it to me. But before we get into the meat of this message, let me offer this advice. Remember that if you are just beginning to learn, take baby steps at first. Crawl before you run.

Now get ready to look at some easy, practical principles of walking in the Spirit that I believe can very well revolutionize your life and change all your tomorrows, forever.

1

you gotta have faith

One time long ago, when I was a young art director for the Kenneth Hagin ministry in Tulsa, Oklahoma, my boss, Billye Brimm, came into my office with a brochure. "Here," she said. "There's a graphic arts seminar at the University of Oklahoma that might interest you. The only thing is, if you want to go, you'll have to go on your own time because it's on a Saturday."

Well, I made plans to go. I marked my calendar for January 11, as I recall. On the evening of the tenth, I set my alarm to get up at five o'clock. I wanted to get an early start for the eighty-mile drive from Tulsa.

Early that morning, about 3 or 4 A.M., I felt my body rock gently, as if I were yet a boy and my dad was waking me up with his hand on my shoulder. I was barely awake when I heard an inner voice say, "Don't go to Oklahoma City today."

I opened my eyes and said, "Okay, Lord, I won't go to Oklahoma City today." Right then I knew it was the Holy Spirit.

"Good," I heard Him say. "Go back to sleep."

"Thank You, Lord; that's so sweet...."

Before I dozed off, I noticed that freezing rain was pelting my window. My last thought was, *God didn't want me driving in an ice storm. How nice.*

A few hours later I awakened with a start. Something was wrong. The sun was shining. The ice storm had come and gone.

I panicked. What about the seminar? *There's no reason for me not to go, I thought. The ice has melted. Was that God last night? Maybe it was a lying spirit trying to make me miss my seminar. Okay, think! I'm going to go to work Monday, and they'll ask, "How was the seminar?" I'm going to say, "Uh, I didn't go. Why? Well, this voice told me not to go."*

They'll say, "Right! A voice told you not to go? We have a nut designing 'The Word of Faith' magazine. You're fired."

My carnal mind kicked in, and I decided, *Okay, I'll miss the first session, but at least I'll make the last three. I don't care if that was God last night. I'm going anyway.* So off I went.

Halfway there I hit the back end of the ice storm. The sleet was so bad that it was a challenge just to stay on the highway. Cars spun off the road, and trailer trucks jackknifed. It was a harrowing drive, but I was more than halfway there and I wasn't going to turn around, come hell or high water.

I pressed on, but soon my windshield wipers went bad and I couldn't see. So I stopped and bought new ones.

Neither wind nor rain nor ice was going to keep me from going to this seminar—I'm a faith-man.

When I arrived in Oklahoma City, I got lost. It took me another half hour to find the campus, then a parking space, then the building where the seminar was supposed to be. At last, I was standing outside of Building A, Room 201, gasping for breath. I had run across the campus and up the stairs.

I hate being late, and I was thinking, *Everyone is going to look at me when I come in. Oh well, suck it up, faith-man.*

I took a breath and opened the door. To my surprise, the room was empty! I closed the door and looked at my brochure. It said Room 201, and that was Room 201. So I opened the door again. Still empty!

Then I had an idea. Maybe the brochure had a misprint. I'm an artist. I've made misprints. Maybe they meant Room 301. So I checked it out. No, it was empty, too. Well, maybe they meant 101. No, empty, too. Finally, I asked some students, "Do you know anything about a graphics art seminar? No? Okay, thanks."

I walked outside and sat on a bench. "All right, Holy Spirit. Something's not right. You don't miss it; people do. So, I'm going to sit down and pray until You tell me what's going on. Where am I missing it?"

I had prayed in the Spirit no more than thirty seconds when I heard the Holy Spirit say (in my spirit), "Look at your brochure."

I was a little reluctant to do that because I had already looked at it a dozen times; but just to appease Him, I did it again.

Let's see, place? University of Oklahoma. Check. Room? Two zero one. Check. Day? Saturday. Check. Date? February 11! Dear God! I'm thirty days too early. This is January; it's not until next month. I felt like an idiot, and I started beating myself up. *Of all the ignorant, stupid, dimwitted...*

But the Holy Spirit interrupted me and said, "Larry, last night, whose voice was it that you heard?"

I was a little sheepish, "Um, Yours?"

"Yes, Mine. Do you remember what My voice sounded like?"

"Uh huh."

"Okay, never forget My voice." And let me tell you, I've never forgotten His voice.

It is a well-known fact that every person has a unique voiceprint, like a thumbprint. No two are alike. We can identify family, friends, and even celebrities (whom we don't know personally) by the sound of their voice alone.

Wouldn't it be silly if your mother called you on the phone and asked you to come for a visit, and you said, "Who is this? Identify yourself! How do I know you're my mother?"

Her next phone call would probably be to get you professional help. Besides, it would hurt her feelings.

Do you suppose it blesses the Lord when we've been with Him for years and still don't know His voice?

walk by faith

On the way back to Tulsa, the Lord spoke to me about my fiasco. He said, "Don't take it so hard. You're learning. But you did hear My voice, and you knew it, until you became double-minded. You started looking at the circumstances, and your carnal mind took over. Next time you'll do better."

That story is a classic example of walking in the Spirit, which simply means being guided and assisted by God. Hearing His voice in our spirit is one of the ways He helps and directs us. You could say that walking in the Spirit is being mindful of the things of God more so than the natural circumstances; it is often walking by faith, not by sight. (2 Cor. 5:7.) When you're spiritually-minded, walking in the Spirit is really not hard, if you know a few things.

First, you have to know that you are capable of walking in the Spirit; every believer is. Here are two scriptural proofs, one from the Old Testament and one from the New Testament:

> *The spirit of man is the candle of the Lord, searching all the inward parts of the belly.*
>
> PROVERBS 20:27

> *Now we have received, not the spirit of the world, but the spirit which is of God; that we might know the things that are freely given to us of God.*
>
> 1 CORINTHIANS 2:12

Second, know that it takes faith to walk in the Spirit. Faith is merely having confidence in the Word of God. You must allow God's Word to be the supreme authority in your life, commit yourself to be guided by it, and trust it more than you do your senses or the opinions of others. That comes from daily Bible reading and meditating on Scriptures. (Rom. 10:17.) If the Word says that you can walk in the Spirit (and it does), then you can.

We just saw how walking in the Spirit involves hearing God's still, small voice in our hearts. (1 Kings 19:12.) Jesus said, "My sheep hear my voice, and I know them, and they follow me" (John 10:27).

Are you a child of God? Is Jesus your Shepherd? Then, according to Jesus, you know His voice and you can follow Him. You can affirm that by repeating aloud, "I have a Shepherd who leads me. I am one of His sheep. I *do* know His voice, and I *do* follow Him."

a learning process

In my opinion, being led by the Spirit is more of an art than a science. You'll make mistakes. Everyone does. But that's not an excuse for being haphazard. You should do the best you can and try to improve daily.

If you do make a mistake, make sure it's out of ignorance and not out of rebellion. It's not as bad when you're wrong, if your heart is right.

When you make miss-steps, correct your error, mend and adjust, then get going again. When you stumble or fall, don't lie there crying, "Help! I've fallen down, and I can't get up." The Word of God says, "For a just man falleth seven times, and riseth up again..." (Prov. 24:16). Pick yourself up, dust yourself off, and get back in the saddle.

Walking in the Spirit is a learning process. The more you do it, the better you will become at it. Soon it will become your first nature. Just allow yourself time to grow.

Sometimes fear of missing God keeps believers from stepping out on a word from Him. Fear is the enemy to walking in the Spirit. Remember this, *"You can't mess things up so badly that God can't fix them."*

The steps of a good man are ordered by the Lord: and he delighteth in his way. Though he fall, he shall not be utterly cast down: for the Lord upholdeth him with his hand.

PSALM 37:23,24

What's my point? Don't bet the farm on your first try. When you first begin, practice making Spirit-led decisions in non-critical areas. That way if you make a mistake, it won't cost you your job or your ministry or your life.

Pay attention to both your successes and failures. Learn from them. Failures can teach you as much as success. At least you'll learn what *not* to do!

I learned a lot of things the hard way. Now I look back at some of my Spirit-led adventures and chuckle.

hear and obey

I think many people have a hard time hearing from God because they *have* heard from Him and they didn't like what He was saying. He may have told them something like, "Give a big financial gift to missions," but they thought that surely it was the enemy's voice and responded, "I rebuke you, you lying spirit."

You see, every believer hears from God, but many turn a deaf ear to Him. If they keep tuning Him out because they don't want to hear what He's telling them, then they won't have confidence to hear from Him when they really want to or need to hear from Him. We have to be consistent.

Most people have more confidence in flesh and blood than they do in the Holy Spirit. That's why they go around asking everyone for counsel. Tell me, who can give you better counsel than the Spirit of God?

One time a person told me, "Brother Huggins, I need your counsel but don't tell me to read my Bible and pray!" I said, "Sorry, I can't help you." That kind of thinking is one reason I stopped counseling people long ago. I don't do it anymore, unless it's crisis counseling or bereavement.

You see, all a good counselor can really do is point you towards God. Ultimately, you need to learn to hear from God for yourself (this book can help you). Remember, there's only one Counselor who's always right and is available twenty-four hours a day—the Holy Spirit.

Oral Roberts used to give this advice: "Pray until you hear from God, confer no more with flesh and blood, obey God at all cost."

The better acquainted you are with God and the more you know His Word, the better results you'll have hearing from Him. The better results you have, the more confidence you'll have. The more confidence you have, the bolder you will be. Eventually, you will learn to recognize the Holy Spirit's voice. When you learn to hear from Him, be sure to instantly obey Him, immediately responding in faith to His guidance within you.

But for now, "Prove all things; hold fast that which is good" (1 Thess. 5:21). The bottom line is, practice makes perfect.

Now, let's get down to where the rubber meets the road.

2

love the truth

Sometimes God speaks in an inward voice, sometimes in an audible voice (although I think the audible voice is rare). But most often, God communicates with us through His written Word and the witness of the Spirit.

Many times the witness of the Spirit is a *silent witness*. What I am saying is, God often communicates directly to our recreated human spirit (2 Cor. 5:17) in a non-verbal manner. Haven't you ever had the experience where you just knew something? You didn't know how you knew it, but you just knew it. I think everyone has had that experience at least once, especially parents.

Or perhaps you've been praying and suddenly a Scripture comes to mind that is the answer to your need or fills you with peace and assurance that everything's going to be all right.

God also leads us as much (or more) by what He doesn't say. What He doesn't say is just as important as what He does say.

Then there's what the old timers used to call a *no*—"a check in the spirit." They might say, "I asked God about something, but I got a check in my spirit," referring to a sense or knowing that they shouldn't do something or go somewhere.

We need to learn to train ourselves to recognize non-verbal (as well as verbal) communications from the Holy Spirit. Sometimes they are faint impressions, easily missed, but we can learn to recognize them. In this book you will be taught how.

It's a challenge to teach on spiritual subjects, especially in book form. We find ourselves searching for examples that won't be misunderstood. We need a common vocabulary. Paul had the same challenge.

> *Which things also we speak, not in the words which man's wisdom teacheth, but which the Holy Ghost teacheth; comparing spiritual things with spiritual.*
>
> 1 CORINTHIANS 2:13

Or, as *The New International Version* says, "...expressing spiritual truths in spiritual words."

Before you can walk in the Spirit with any accuracy or consistency, you must become a lover of truth. This is fundamental. It may seem simple, but it's powerful. Walking in the Spirit is walking in truth, absolute truth. It goes without saying that this requires you to maintain a Word-based lifestyle (as the Word and the truth are interchangeable). But this is more than merely tolerating the truth; it's loving the truth, even when it hurts. The Holy Spirit is the Spirit of truth—absolute truth.

Howbeit when he, the Spirit of truth, is come, he will guide you into all truth: for he shall not speak of himself; but whatsoever he shall hear, that shall he speak: and he will shew you things to come.

JOHN 16:13

The Holy Spirit can only lead you into truth. He cannot lead you into error. That's impossible. When we get into error, we do it on our own.

My old friend Mother Grace Tucker (who's been in ministry for many years) used to say, "The Holy Ghost don't miss it. We're the ones that miss it."

The Holy Spirit isn't the spirit of tradition or the spirit of political correctness or the spirit of what you want to hear. He's the Spirit of truth; He only bears witness of the truth.

A well-known Christian demographer claims that more than 80 percent of the Christians he polled do not believe in the concept of absolute truth.

What do they believe in? *Relativism,* a term meaning, "A view that ethical truths depend on the individuals and groups holding them."[1] That's why one year a denomination is against same-sex marriages, and the next year they vote to solemnize same-sex marriages.

Who changed? God? No, they gave in to public pressure. They became politically correct.

The Holy Spirit doesn't have to agree with your church creed, your mama, or the Supreme Court. He agrees with the Word of God. (John 16:13.)

You need to love the truth and embrace it, even if it hurts. The truth isn't always easy; it's double-edged.

> *For the word of God is living and active. Sharper than any double–edged sword, it penetrates even to dividing soul and spirit, joints and marrow; it judges the thoughts and attitudes of the heart.*
>
> HEBREWS 4:12 NIV

You won't walk very far with the Holy Spirit if you only want to hear what you want to hear, what makes you feel good, and what always casts you in the best light. That's like the man whose doctor told him he was overweight. He said, "I'd like a second opinion."

"Fine with me," said his doctor. "You're ugly, too!"

Some people won't go to a church where the pastor preaches the truth. They have itching ears; they only want them to be tickled with pretty sermons. Sons of God—believers who are led by the Spirit (John 1:12; Rom. 8:14)—don't run from the truth; they run to the truth. When the pastor pins their ears to the wall by preaching a truth-based message that hits home, they say, "Thank you, Pastor; I needed that."

The truth stands on its own. The apostle Paul put it this way: "For we can do nothing against the truth, but for the truth" (2 Cor. 13:8).

Truth is not influenced by public opinion. In fact, it's often unpopular. So be careful of following the crowd; they can take you to hell.

Jesus said, "Enter ye in at the strait gate: for wide is the gate, and broad is the way, that leadeth to destruction, and many there be which go in thereat" (Matt. 7:13). In the very next verse He said it's the minority who stand a better chance of being right, "Because strait is the gate, and narrow is the way, which leadeth unto life, and few there be that find it" (v.14).

The problem with many people is a misconception of how things work in the kingdom of God. They don't understand that the church isn't a democracy; it's a theocracy. It's not governed by the people; it's governed by God.

monkey-wrench mentality

Theocracy is government by God. But somewhere along the way, some in the church tried to substitute democratic principles for kingdom principles. Democracy is based upon the assumption that individuals are prone to error and there's safety in numbers. That works fairly well in secular government, but it isn't perfect.

A great man once said, "Democracy is the worst form of government, but so far it's the best we've found." That's not the way God rules. That's the world's method.

Don't misjudge what I'm saying here. I love this democratic republic called the USA, but I believe that democracy in its purest form can lead to anarchy, which consists of lawlessness, confusion, and mob rule. What makes America work is that we are a republic—a constitutional, representative, elected government. Webster's Dictionary defines *republic* as one "in which supreme power resides in a body of citizens entitled to vote and is exercised by elected officers and representatives responsible to them and governing according to law."[2] We are not governed by the mob, but by immutable principles, based upon truth.

It's common knowledge that some in government wait until they see the daily polls before they make their decisions. That's a type of mob rule, is it not? But a true statesman is governed by principles, not by opinions.

In God's kingdom we are governed by the truth of His Word. Our opinion doesn't count because God's Word is perfect; it is truth and doesn't need us to reinterpret it. The simple fact is, if we live by it, things will work right.

But whoso looketh into the perfect law of liberty, and continueth therein, he being not a forgetful hearer, but a doer of the work, this man shall be blessed in his deed.

JAMES 1:25

When opinionated people start tinkering with God's Word, they throw a monkey wrench into the machinery.

They make statements like, "I believe things are this way" or, "Things should be this way." Be careful. Unless beliefs are based upon the Word of God, they're just opinions.

our way or His way?

Someone once showed Kenneth Hagin a Scripture and asked, "What's your opinion about this verse, Brother Hagin?" He answered, "I don't have an opinion; whatever it says is exactly what I believe." He said they looked at him like he had slipped a gear.

This is hard for most to grasp. "No opinion? Why, that's un-American. I got a right to my opinion."

Let me tell you about opinion. In the church, wherever you have two Christians, you have at least three opinions.

Opinions change like the wind. One day we feel like this, another day we feel like that.

Are you really going to base an important decision on someone else's opinion? Their track record may be worse than yours. Besides, can they be as concerned for your welfare as you are?

Human nature being what it is, if you ask someone for advice, they may be so flattered that they might make something up. How many people will be honest enough to say, "Gee, I don't know; maybe you should pray"?

Next time someone offers you advice, ask them if they will guarantee results and assume all the consequences, or the debts, if things don't work out.

I'm glad that God is God because God doesn't change. He's not going to make exceptions to His Word to appease humanity or to be popular. Jesus said, "And blessed is he, whosoever shall not be offended in me" (Luke 7:23). There has to be a fixed point upon which we calibrate our moral compass. Otherwise, the ground is moving under us, and everything is in a constant state of flux.

Well-known performing artist Frank Sinatra's anthem was, "I did it my way." I wonder where that took him? All my way ever did was get me in trouble.

walk, don't run

When I was a freshman in college, I wasn't very political. I was a fine arts student, and I wore my hair long. That's back in the days when our university had few long-haired students.

Well, one day a professor invited me to his house and I was flattered, until I caught on to why he had invited me. He was a Communist, and he had invited about eighteen campus radicals to his house for a rap session. I wasn't a Communist. I was a sculptor!

I listened as these young intellectuals argued the merits of Maoism verses Stalinism, Socialism verses Communism, Trotskyism verses Leninism. One guy even looked like the infamous revolutionary leader Che Guevara,[3] from his boots and fatigues to his beard and beret.

At one point I thought there would be a fistfight. I was just hoping it would all be over before they asked me a question.

Too late. The professor reeled me in. "Mr. Huggins, what's your opinion? Communism or Socialism?"

I begged out. "Uh, I dunno. You better ask someone else."

"No, you've been listening all evening. What do you think?"

"Well," I said meekly, "I think you're all wrong. I don't believe in Communism or Socialism. I'm not even sure democracy is the best government because I don't think people were meant to govern themselves. What we need is a benevolent King; we can be His sheep and live pastoral lives."

They looked at me like I had just fallen from a turnip truck. At least, they never tried to recruit me again.

I was nineteen years old at the time. These many years later, I still believe the world needs a benevolent King. His name is Jesus, and the government should be upon His shoulders, not on the shoulders of flawed human beings. The Bible assures us that one day it will be like that.

> *For unto us a child is born, unto us a son is given: and the government shall be upon his shoulder: and his name shall be called Wonderful, Counselor, The mighty God, The everlasting Father, The Prince of Peace.*
>
> ISAIAH 9:6

Now, I'm not being unpatriotic. I believe that even though we Christians are not of this world (John 17:14), we are citizens of our country and should operate in and exercise the freedoms we are given. Did you know that the Bible instructs us to pray for those in leadership in our government and to pray for our land? (1 Tim. 2:1-2; 2 Chron. 7:14.) Praying for our leaders, praying for godly wisdom and solutions for issues that arise in this nation, is every Christian's responsibility. But I'm explaining why I think that majority rule doesn't work in the economy of God.

You and I, right now, as believers, live in the kingdom of God. We live by kingdom principles. In this kingdom we are not moved by public opinion; the Spirit of truth moves us. We don't run with the crowd; we walk in the Spirit.

They are not of the world, even as I am not of the world.
Sanctify them through thy truth: thy word is truth.

JOHN 17:16,17

Here's one last sobering thought concerning the Spirit of truth. If we are not yielding to the Spirit of truth, then what are we yielding to? In the world there are two spirits that are in diametric opposition: the Spirit of truth, and the spirit of iniquity (or "malice, evil purposes and desires"⁴). There's no middle ground. With God, it's always black or white.

For the mystery of iniquity doth already work: only he who now letteth will let, until he be taken out of the way.

And then shall that Wicked be revealed, whom the Lord shall consume with the spirit of his mouth, and shall destroy with the brightness of his coming:

Even him, whose coming is after the working of Satan with all power and signs and lying wonders,

And with all deceivableness of unrighteousness in them that perish; because they received not the love of the truth, that they might be saved.

And for this cause God shall send them strong delusion, that they should believe a lie:

That they all might be damned who believed not the truth, but had pleasure in unrighteousness.

2 THESSALONIANS 2:7-12

Notice verse 10 says they perished "...because they received not the love of the truth...." Truth lasts forever, and they who are steadfast in the truth are preserved by truth. Contrariwise, those who build upon spurious beliefs are destined to fail in the end.

little foxes spoil the vines

In 2 Timothy 3:13, the apostle Paul warned Timothy that in the last days, deception would be epidemic. "But evil men and seducers shall wax worse and worse, deceiving, and being deceived."

Notice he said, "deceiving, and being deceived." There's a saying I've heard since I was a child. "You can't kid an old kidder." Have you ever heard that? Nothing could be further from the truth. Deceivers are the most vulnerable to being deceived.

How do bank tellers learn to spot counterfeit banknotes? They handle large quantities of genuine banknotes, day in and day out. They get used to the real thing. They know how a real bill feels, how it folds, how it wears. Then, when a phony banknote gets into their hands, it sets off an inner alarm.

So it is with people who deal with truth. They recognize truth. They have a sense of how truth strikes their spirit. When something untrue is presented to them, it sets off an inner alarm. But people who deal in deception don't have a feel for the truth.

Become a lover of truth. Desire the truth. Celebrate the truth, even if it cuts both ways. And heed this warning: Be far removed from telling lies, even little, white lies.

Some believe that little lies are harmless and justified if it avoids hurting someone. That's another example of relativism, or situational ethics. No, lies are inexcusable under any circumstance. They ultimately cause damage.

Little lies are like "the little foxes, that spoil the vines" (Song 2:15). They can eventually destroy one's confidence. We're told in the Bible that we should speak the truth in love. (Eph. 4:15.) God has shown us that there's a right way and a wrong way to speak.

Once a friend told me how she responds to the question, "What do you think of my baby?" That comes up a lot, right? Honestly, some newborns, as precious as they are, just don't look cute; they're downright homely. What do you say, "Egad, lady, what an ugly baby"?

So my friend smiles and says, "Now, that's what I call a real baby!" Well, that's speaking the truth in love, isn't it?

If you find yourself in a situation where you don't know what to say, here's the best way to deal with it: either zip your lip, or pray for wisdom before you speak.

it's fundamental

Jesus knew how to answer hard questions. One time a group of religious bigots cornered Him and tried to trip Him up by asking, "By what authority doest thou these things? or who is he that gave thee this authority?" (Luke 20:1,2).

Jesus answered their question with a question (you can do that too).

> *And he answered and said unto them, I will also ask you one thing; and answer me:*
> *The baptism of John, was it from heaven, or of men?*
> LUKE 20:3,4

Did you see how Jesus turned the tables on them? Don't you love Him?

> *They discussed it among themselves and said, "If we say, 'From heaven,' he will ask, 'Why didn't you believe him?'*
> *But if we say, 'From men,' all the people will stone us, because they are persuaded that John was a prophet."*
> *So they answered, "We don't know where it was from."*
> LUKE 20:5-7 NIV

Take a lesson from Jesus—you don't have to answer baited questions.

And Jesus said unto them, Neither tell I you by what authority I do these things.

LUKE 20:8

Honesty is always the best policy. Lies will always catch up with the liar. Never sow things you don't want to reap. Lies will bite you.

In the book of Job in the Old Testament, Job's friend warned, "Even as I have seen, they that plow iniquity, and sow wickedness, reap the same" (Job 4:8).

Yes, you're going to reap what you sow (Gal. 6:7); that's a promise. Besides, telling the truth is easier than lying. You don't have the pressure of keeping your stories straight or remembering what you said to whom.

What does this have to do with walking in the Spirit? Everything; it's fundamental. Remember, the Holy Spirit is the Spirit of truth. The more truth you have in you, the more you hold to the truth, and the easier it is for Him to lead you.

I know that I could lose you as a reader with the kind of teaching in this chapter, but if you get through this book, I believe you're going to receive information that will ultimately change your life.

3

tune your instrument

If you've ever been around old-time Pentecostals, you've probably heard someone declare, with a neck-jerk, "My God, I *feeeel* the witness of the Spirit!" Then they might run their tickling fingers up their arm to indicate the presence of goose bumps.

Hey, I can snap my neck with the best of them, and I get goose bumps sometimes; many believers do, I guess. But that's not necessarily the witness of the Spirit.

As one old preacher said, "I ain't sure what the anointing is, but I'm sure when it ain't!" Likewise, it's sometimes difficult to express what the witness of the Spirit is, but it's obvious when there is no witness.

In this chapter we're going to delve into the witness of the Spirit. Did you know that one meaning of *witness* has to do with testifying or giving evidence? Before we continue, I want you to read two verses of Scripture about the inner witness; then I'll shed some light on them.

The Spirit itself beareth witness with our spirit, that we are the children of God.

ROMANS 8:16

I say the truth in Christ, I lie not, my conscience also bearing me witness in the Holy Ghost.

ROMANS 9:1

The word for *witness* here in the New Testament Greek is "summartureo" (soom-mar-too-reh'-o), which means to testify *jointly*, to corroborate by concurrent evidence, or to sound together.[1] It is used interchangeably in the *King James Version* as "testify unto" or "bear witness with."[2] A legal word, it always refers to requiring two or more witnesses, jointly providing corroborating evidence. In a moment we'll see how God does that with us through His Word and His Spirit.

I've heard people use the following verse on *witness* out of context. In 2 Corinthians 13:1, the apostle Paul said, "...In the mouth of two or three witnesses shall every word be established." Some Bible teachers have taken that verse to mean that they need to have at least two witnesses, or Scriptures, to prove a doctrine, and that's what they do—they put two Scriptures together and call it a doctrine.

Be careful! I can find two Scriptures that seem to say that going naked is okay. Forget that! But you get my point, right?

Actually, in that verse Paul was referring back to Deuteronomy 19:15, which says that if anyone is accused of committing a sin, the accuser must produce a minimum of two eyewitnesses who can prove their case against the accused sinner.

The *New Life Version* of 2 Corinthians 13:1 says it this way: "The Holy Writings tell us that when people think someone has done wrong, it must be proven by two or three people *who saw the wrong being done.*" Let me give you an example.

Once, a church member approached me warily. "Oh, Brother Huggins, I have bad news, but I don't know how to say it."

"Just spit it out," I said.

"But it's about one of your ministers."

"What about him?" I asked.

"Well, I saw him coming out of a beer joint on Archer Street."

"Ha!" I laughed. "Good! The last time the Holy Spirit led him into a bar on Archer Street he stopped a fight and got a man saved. He had him outside on his knees, praying for salvation."

Then I said, "Now, I hope you learn a lesson from this. Be careful what you say about someone else; don't take things by the wrong handle."

Let me tell you, if you see a deacon getting drunk in a Karaoke bar, wearing a pink tutu, singing and dancing atop a table like James Brown—forget about it! You shouldn't bring an accusation against him unless you can produce another eyewitness to back up your story. (Even then, consider approaching him about the matter first, privately, before accusing him to someone in higher authority as that church member did to me. Maybe find out if something is going on in his life that has made him act that way, and see if you can help.)

That may be an extreme example, but the point is, one person cannot bear witness against someone else. That's also true about bearing witness of himself—not even Jesus can do that!

bearing witness

If I bear witness of myself, my witness is not true.

There is another that beareth witness of me; and I know that the witness which he witnesseth of me is true.

JOHN 5:31,32

To *bear witness* of yourself means to testify, say, or affirm that you have seen or heard or experienced something, or that you know it because you were taught by divine revelation or inspiration.[3] In verse 32 Jesus was referring to God the Father and to others who testified of who He is. Later, He said that His works bore witness and the heavenly Father bore witness that He was sent by His Father and was the Son of God. (John 5:36,37.)

If Jesus, who is "the faithful witness" (Rev. 1:5), the Truth itself,[4] wouldn't bear witness of Himself, we certainly must not bear witness of ourselves.

We need a corroborating witness to confirm that we are on the right path. I'm talking about the witness of the Holy Spirit within us. Without that witness we are merely being self-ruled.

We already saw that God doesn't usually lead us by dreams and visions, although He does occasionally operate that way. No, one of the main ways He leads us is by the inner witness of the Spirit, who is, as we learned, the Spirit of truth.

> *"...it is the Spirit that beareth witness, because the Spirit is truth."*
>
> 1 JOHN 5:6

Let me paraphrase this verse: It is the Holy Spirit who furnishes corroborating evidence jointly with our born-again human spirit (which is in union with God), because the Holy Spirit is the Spirit of absolute truth.

Okay, let's review for a moment. What does the Holy Spirit bear witness of? Truth, Bible truth, absolute truth, and nothing but the truth.

Can the Holy Spirit bear witness of a falsehood? No. Can He bear witness of heresy? No. Can He bear witness of your opinion? Not unless you happen to be in agreement with the Word of God.

Can people bear witness for us? In some cases yes, but we don't want to be people-led; we want to be Spirit-led. Now I'm not saying that you should go to your pastor and say, "Brother Huggins says that I don't have to listen to you anymore." That's not what I said. Truth is truth, and the Holy Spirit might be speaking to you through your pastor.

When you are Spirit-led, the Holy Spirit will bear witness when others are giving you godly counsel. We can trust the counsel of people who know how to hear from God and who are sold out to the truth. But, please remember, people are fallible. That's why Jesus sent us *another Counselor* (John 14:16 NLV)—the Holy Spirit.

Can people bear false witness? Yes, and they often do. Can they be confused? Yes, and many times they are. Can they be deceived? Yes, they can.

I'm not judging anyone's heart. They may be very sincere but sincerely wrong. Nevertheless, they're still wrong, and two wrongs never make a right.

> *And he spake a parable unto them, Can the blind lead the blind? shall they not both fall into the ditch?*
>
> LUKE 6:39

The witness of any person, friend, family member, pastor, priest, or counselor is always subject to being judged in the light of God's Word and by the trying of the spirits.[5]

> *Beloved, believe not every spirit, but try the spirits whether they are of God: because many false prophets are gone out into the world.*
>
> 1 JOHN 4:1

To *try the spirits* is "to test, examine, prove, scrutinise (to see whether a thing is genuine or not)...."[6] It means that utterances can be true, inspired by the Holy Spirit, or utterances can be spurious, inspired by another type of motivation. But keep in mind that even godly people occasionally miss it. We should judge the utterance, not the person.

Some people are more reliable witnesses than others. That's why I hope you have the good sense to pick a pastor who is born again, Spirit-led, and preaches Word-based messages, and to surround yourself with godly people.

We already looked at truth in the last chapter, but we're going to cover one more aspect of truth and the inner witness next because it relates to staying in tune with the Spirit.

ring of truth

I often use the phrase "ring of truth" to express the witness of the Spirit. I'm not talking about an audible sound, but a spiritual quality. Let me describe this spiritual truth with a musical example.

When I was in physical science class, in grade school, the teacher gave a demonstration I never forgot. Maybe you've seen this too.

He used two identical tuning forks. He struck one, and we all heard the clear tone it produced. Then he held the second tuning fork near the first, and the second rang just like the first. In fact, the sound seemed to be amplified. There was a sympathetic relationship between the two instruments. Because they were both tuned to the same key, each affected the other.

My understanding of how this phenomenon works is that the first tuning fork vibrates at a precise frequency. It moves air molecules and produces sound waves. The sound waves strike the second tuning fork, and it begins to vibrate. Because it's pre-tuned to the same frequency as the first, it vibrates at the same frequency and produces the same tone.

This won't work, I am told, if the tuning forks are in different keys.

Here's the analogy I'm drawing. The Holy Spirit is tuned to the key of *truth*. It rings with the Word of God. If we will tune our born-again, recreated human spirit (which is in union with God) to the key of truth, it will ring whenever it comes in contact with truth. The point is, if your heart isn't tuned to truth, it won't recognize the witness of the Spirit.

You could say then that when you're walking in the Spirit, you're in tune with the Spirit; you're walking in symphony with Him. He can "play" upon your heartstrings because you have tuned them to the truth of His Word. So the witness of the Spirit is like a sounding together, or furnishing of corroborating evidence. It's agreement, or symphony.

Again I say unto you, That if two of you shall agree on earth as touching any thing that they shall ask, it shall be done for them of my Father which is in heaven.

MATTHEW 18:19

The operative word here is *agree*. Of course, the context here is agreeing with your prayer partners, but I want you to look at the principle of agreement, so you can get into agreement with God. How can you walk with God if you're not in agreement with His will (which is His Word)?

Can two walk together, except they be agreed?

AMOS 3:3

The New Testament Greek word for *agreement* is "sumphoneo," meaning "to sound together...to be in accord...."[7] It's a musical term; you may recognize it as being the root of *symphony.* So then, to be in agreement is to sound together, to symphonize, or to be in accord.

Disagreement, then, would be *not* saying the same thing; it would be disharmony or discord.

When singers harmonize it makes a pleasing sound and beautiful music. When singers are in discord, it is unpleasant and uncomfortable.

You don't have to be a trained musician to recognize good, harmonious music. Most people seem to have a sense for it. Likewise, we know noise and disharmony when we hear it.

In the same way, we should be able to recognize when we're in harmony with God or in disharmony with God. When we become born again,[8] we have all the spiritual equipment to recognize His presence and hear His voice. We just need to train ourselves to tune in to His Spirit (you'll learn one way in the next section). When you are tuned in to Him, you are in harmony with God. The more you experience that kind of harmony, the quicker you will spot discordance.

36

I feel sorry for some people. Their lives ar
and so chaotic that they seldom experience peace ҩ
harmony. It's difficult for them to hear from God because of
the distractions in their life. Strife and pain have a way of
demanding attention. It's difficult to hear from God when
others are screaming for attention. It's like trying to tune a
violin in a steel mill.

pray until you know

We just saw that when we are born again, our human
spirit (our instrument) is in tune to the key of truth. With
that in mind, let me tell you how to keep your instrument
tuned. First of all, get into the Word and stay there; read and
meditate on it daily. That should go without saying. But you
also have to pray in the Spirit— the more the better.

Praying in the Spirit tunes our born-again spirit to the
Holy Spirit.

If you don't have your prayer language, I strongly encourage you to seek God for it. Ask Him to give it to you in the
same way you asked Jesus into your heart to become born
again. Then by faith begin to speak out any sounds or sylla-
bles that you feel rise up inside you (there may be only a few
at first). Sometimes it doesn't happen right away. If this is the
case for you, don't be discouraged. Just receive it by faith and
keep trying until it happens.

Praying in the Spirit is of paramount importance. Remember what Peter said about the gift of the Holy Ghost being for everyone? "For the promise is unto you, and to your children, and to all that are afar off, even as many as the Lord our God shall call" (Acts 2:38,39).

He gives the utterances in our spirit, but we must speak them out as we are prompted.

Without your prayer language you will have a difficult time staying in harmony with the Holy Spirit. You'll be moved by your feelings and thoughts instead of by His witness.

Now we have received, not the spirit of the world, but the spirit which is of God; that we might know the things that are freely given to us of God.

1 CORINTHIANS 2:12

When we pray out of our intellect, we pray what we know. Most often, we know the problem so naturally we begin by praying the problem. We tell God everything we're going through. For instance, "Oh, God, do you see what they are doing to me at work? They're persecuting me. I'm going to lose my job. If I lose my job, I'll lose my car. If I lose my car, I can't go to church, I can't pay tithes, and I'll set the kingdom of God back at least a hundred years! Oh God..."

That's not prayer; it's murmuring and complaining. Aren't murmuring and complaining what kept the children of Israel wandering through the wilderness for forty years?

We need to pray the answer, not the problem.

"But, I don't know the answer," you may say.

Aha! That's why you need to pray in tongues. The Holy Spirit has your answer. Yield to Him; let Him pray your answer through you.

> *Likewise the Spirit also helpeth our infirmities: for we know not what we should pray for as we ought: but the Spirit itself maketh intercession for us with groanings which cannot be uttered.*
>
> *And he that searcheth the hearts knoweth what is the mind of the Spirit, because he maketh intercession for the saints according to the will of God.*
>
> *And we know that all things work together for good to them that love God, to them who are the called according to his purpose.*
>
> ROMANS 8:26-28

What does that say in plain speech? It says that when we don't know how to pray, we need to pray in other tongues, allowing the Holy Spirit, who knows God's will for us, to search everything thoroughly, until we have a sense of knowing that it's all going to work out right.

Here's an even more simplified meaning: When you don't know, pray in the Spirit until you do know.

How long should you pray, five minutes, an hour, two hours? Pray until you know. That could be thirty seconds or ten hours; it could be a short amount of time or a longer amount of time. But pray until you know it's all going to work out according to God's will.

stay in harmony

Let's assume you are a Spirit-filled believer who speaks in tongues (if you're still not, I encourage you to put down this book, start worshipping God, follow the information on receiving your prayer language in the previous section, and don't stop until you are praying in tongues). Okay, so you're a Spirit-filled believer and you start praying in your prayer language—not English or a foreign language—maybe something like "Shandalala..." (use your imagination here).

At first it may take effort, but keep with it. Your mind will probably be active; all sorts of thoughts may be rattling around inside your head: *What about lunch? Did I feed the dog? What's on TV? Is anyone listening to me?* Keep praying in tongues anyway.

It may seem to be as dry as corn shucks. Keep praying anyway. Your prayer language may sound goofy to you. Keep praying anyway. Eventually, your mind will become quiet, your prayer language will get stronger, and you'll hit a divine flow (or have a steady stream of Spirit-inspired words pouring out of your mouth).

Stay in that flow. Your born-again human spirit, which is in union with God, will begin to harmonize with the Holy Spirit. The more you do this, the more you'll be in tune with Him.

One important thing to remember is that the Holy Spirit will always say what the Word says. They will never disagree. The Holy Spirit will never lead anyone to do anything that is in conflict to the Bible. Learn this now, and learn it well. Always test your intuitions with the Word of God. If they don't agree with what's written in the Book, ignore them.

For there are three that bear record in heaven, the Father, the Word, and the Holy Ghost: and these three are one.

1 JOHN 5:7

The phrase *three that bear record in heaven* can be translated, *three that agree in heaven.*[8] Or, I could say, three that testify jointly, who sound together concurrently, with corroborating evidence.

I've seen many people who think they are being led by the Spirit, but they can't be because their actions are in conflict with the Word. They may be borderline psychotics! Or they're being deceived by a lying spirit (or both). But most likely they don't really know the easy way to be Spirit-led. Remember, the Holy Spirit only leads in harmony with the written Word of God.

Let's look back at what we've learned so far. Number one, you must love the truth, even if it hurts. Number two, the Holy Spirit is the Spirit of Truth. Number three, the witness of the Spirit is a sounding together, or furnishing of corroborating evidence. Number four, you tune your spirit by studying the Word and praying in the Spirit. Number five, when your heart is tuned to God's truth, the witness of the Spirit will ring true in your heart.

If you are clear on these fundamentals, you can go on. If not, re-read this chapter, because there's a practical way to apply what you've discovered, and we're going to look at it now. In the next chapter, we'll get to the heart of the matter and put these truths to work.

4

the secret's in the asking

Call unto me, and I will answer thee, and shew thee great and mighty things, which thou knowest not.

JEREMIAH 33:3

Here is a truth that you must believe to walk in the Spirit easily: When you call upon God, He *will* answer you. Of course, this is a conditional promise.

Then shalt thou call, and the Lord shall answer; thou shalt cry, and he shall say, Here I am. If thou take away from the midst of thee the yoke, the putting forth of the finger, and speaking vanity.

ISAIAH 58:9

So there are hindrances to hearing an answer from God, such as finger pointing, malicious talk, and oppressing others. King David said, "If I regard iniquity in my heart [or enjoy sin[1]], the Lord will not hear me" (Ps. 66:18). You can see from this verse that those hindrances must be removed if you want a clear pathway to God.

If you deal with those problem areas, then you'll have confidence to walk in the Spirit. Removing them begins with repentance, which means changing one's mind for better,[2] or turning from sin to God in faith. If you're unwilling to repent, then give this book to someone who is serious about walking in the Spirit.

Good, I'm glad you mean business. Now, let's get on with the program.

If God's promised to answer when we call, then why are we having such difficulty knowing the answer? The problem is how we ask.

First of all, stop asking God *essay* questions. I have found that God responds in kind. If you ask Him a complicated question, you'll probably get a complicated answer. So if you're confused about something, that may be why.

I discourage people from asking my advice. Why? They usually start by telling me everything that's going on in their lives. Then they tell me what's going on in the lives of everyone around them (or what *they* think is going on). They continue on, telling me about their childhood. Finally, they run down the list of variations of their concerns and all the possible outcomes. They factor in their diet, the phases of the moon, their inherited family traits…. By the time they get through, I've got no clue what their question was. Have you ever done that to God?

If every seed sown produces after its kind, (Gen. 1:11,12), and it does, questions should produce after their kind because they contain the seed of their answer. So if grass brings forth grass, and cattle bring forth cattle, complicated questions produce complicated answers. Likewise, ask a simple question and you're bound to get a simple answer. It all goes back to the kind of seed that is sown.

If you don't learn anything else from this book, learn this: Whenever possible ask God simple questions that can be answered by a simple yes or no.

You've seen this scenario: A young lady has her sights on a cute boy, so she reminds God about his athletic abilities, his parents, his genealogy, and how she can bring out his better qualities if God will allow them to marry. But she should ask, "Lord, is this the one for me, yes or no?" Have you ever known anyone like that? It's a good example of what we're talking about in this chapter.

Keeping it relevant will help you get a timely answer from God.

say what you mean

Jesus said, "But let your communication be, Yea, yea; Nay, nay: for whatsoever is more than these cometh of evil" (Matt.

5:37). *The Message Bible* says it this way, "Just say 'yes' and 'no.' When you manipulate words to get your own way, you go wrong." You have to let yes mean *yes*, and no mean *no*.

Some people say things with their mouth, but they don't mean them sincerely in their hearts. They say yes when they mean no (I've never figured out why). For instance, if you're one of those people who's always committing to things you don't want to do ("Oh sure, I'll watch your 'precious' children [unruly little terrors] tonight"), and you say yes when you mean no, you need to get that fixed! It's like a tee-shirt I saw once that said, "What part of NO don't you understand?"

Well, you never have to be concerned about God's yes and no. When He says yes, He means yes. When He says no, He means no. You don't have to reinterpret it. If you're going to ask God for answers, be willing to accept what He says. If you're going to do what you want to do anyway, leave God out of it.

That's why I'm suspicious of people who run from pastor to pastor asking for advice. If they don't like Pastor Smart's advice, they run to Pastor Wise. If he gives the same advice as Pastor Smart, they keep going until they finally end up with Pastor Dumb, who tells them what they want to hear. So they ignore Smart and Wise, and choose Dumb.

They didn't really have to go through all that. They could have just done what they were going to do in the first place and call it a day.

Once a lady pushed past my secretary, slung my office door open, and declared, "I'm leaving my [expletive deleted] husband! I'm not asking your advice; I'm telling you. I'm leaving him. What do you think about that?"

I said, "What difference does it matter what I think if you've already made up your mind?"

"Good!" she said. "I'm outta here," and she left.

That evening, I got a call from her irate husband demanding to know, "Why did you tell my wife to leave me?"

I told him what really happened, and he said, "That sounds right. She's always trying to get someone to take her side."

God can see through that kind of conniving, manipulative behavior. Get real. Ask Him real questions. What can you expect to hear from Him when you do? Real answers— ideally yes and no answers.

But that's not enough information to go on, you might say. Yes it is, if you ask enough yes and no questions. You're not limited to one question.

Ask, and it shall be given you; seek, and ye shall find; knock, and it shall be opened unto you:

For every one that asketh receiveth; and he that seeketh findeth; and to him that knocketh it shall be opened.

MATTHEW 7:7,8

In other words, ask and keep on asking...knock and keep on knocking.

I'm going to point out two things about asking God questions. When you ask, expect to get an instant reply (yes, instant). If you don't get an instant reply, ask another question, but "ask and keep on asking," and expect Him to answer.

That doesn't mean ask the same question over and over, like a broken record. It used to drive me up the wall when my little boys would ask, "But why? But why? But..."

They'd keep asking that over and over until finally I'd burst out, "Because I said so, that's why!" If you are a parent, I'm sure you can relate.

Don't ask God the same question over and over. Rethink your question. Rephrase it, or ask a different question.

Remember, the Holy Spirit is the Spirit of truth. He responds to truth. He doesn't have to dignify an inappropriate question.

Ye ask, and receive not, because ye ask amiss, that ye may consume it upon your lusts.

JAMES 4:3

Let me say it this way: When you ask and you don't get an answer, it may be because you've asked an inappropriate question (or your motives are wrong). In fact, let's discuss motivation for a moment.

motivating factor

Who in their right mind would try to deceive God? Yet, there are people who ask Him for things with an improper motive and try to trick Him into giving them the answer they want to hear. One Bible commentary says they do this to "have the means of gratifying their sensual desires."[3] Hey, if you want to do something, one excuse is just as good as another. As I said before, leave God out of it if you're going to do it anyway.

And let me insert this. Stop saying, "God told me to do this or that." If He didn't really say it, don't use Him for validation. That's bearing false witness. In the world *bearing false witness* is a legal term referring to making false statements under oath, and it's a criminal offense. In the spiritual realm, bearing false witness about God is a sin (I believe it's worse than cussin' and drinkin'), and it's offensive to God.

Have you had trouble hearing from God lately? I'm sure that you never have trouble with your motives, so the problem must be that you've asked the wrong question.

That's easy to fix. Ask another question. Still no answer? Ask another question.

You see, the secret is in the asking. Remember, every *appropriate* question contains the seed of its own answer. Put some thought into questioning your questions beforehand. Then when you ask a true question, or a question that's based upon truth, you should get an immediate response.

Two things to remember: Ask *appropriate* questions, and ask *simple* questions that can be answered with a simple *yes* or *no*.

getting the clear picture

Did you ever play the game Twenty Questions? I often do that with God. "Lord, do You want me to preach? Teach? Minister in the Spirit? Word of Wisdom? Gift of Healing? To men? To one man? Will I know him when I see him? Is it healing? Is it his stomach? Is it cancer? In the beginning of the service? At the end? Will he be seated near the front? In the back?"

You get the picture. When you ask the appropriate question, you can instantly get a *yes* or a *no* in your spirit (but remember, if this doesn't happen, rephrase the question and keep asking). When you need more information, ask more questions.

Once, I asked God one hundred and forty-four questions (I counted them), one after the other. I was relocating my home and ministry, and I didn't want to miss God. Here's a hypothetical scenario of a question and answer series.

"Oh, Lord, do I have a ministry, yes or no?"

[Yes]

"Am I going to be in full-time ministry?"

[Yes]

"Do You want me to quit my job?"

[No]

"Will I begin my ministry this year?"

[No]

"Will I begin my ministry after this year?"

[No]

"Will I begin right away?"

[Yes]

"Will I begin in this church?"

[Yes]

"Is it in the pulpit?"

[No]

"Youth minister?"

[No]

"Children's church?"

[No]

"It's not cleaning toilets, is it?"

[TaDa!]

"Do I begin this morning?"

[TaDa!]

"Is this You, God?"

[Hal-le-lu-jah, Hal-le-lu-jah!]

Each time you get a yes or a no from the Spirit, you get a fragment of information, like a pixel of information you might see in a digital image. The more individual pixels you get, the clearer the picture becomes. Don't get one pixel and run off half-cocked.

> *The entrance of thy words giveth light; it giveth understanding unto the simple.*
>
> PSALM 119:130

If you walk through a dark room, you walk slowly, groping, testing each step. When the lights come on, you can run through the room. Likewise, go slow in asking God questions, if necessary, until you have enough light to run.

However, I need to caution you again. Please, start out with non-critical issues if you're still learning the process. Take baby steps. If you miss it, mend and adjust.

number one priority

Be sure to pray a lot, too, and pray overtime. And remember that you don't have to go with your first impression. For example, you could pray about something for several days, and if each day the answer keeps coming up *yes*, then you can be relatively sure you're on track (maybe).

The bottom line is, get out of the mental realm and out of the emotional realm, and get into the spiritual realm, the realm of truth—"walk not after the flesh, but after the Spirit" (Rom. 8:4). Don't play games with God. Make hearing from Him your number one priority.

Going about this half-heartedly is asking for trouble. Your safety net is spiritual integrity, so if you haven't been putting your whole heart into it, I encourage you to check your motivation and get serious about hearing from God now. Don't wait until it becomes a matter of life and death for you to be motivated. But I'm sure that if you do, you'll be motivated quickly!

As you become more honest, serious, and sincere about hearing from God, your success at recognizing when you receive the inner witness of the Spirit will improve. Build upon your successes. As you become more proficient, you'll gain confidence. Then you can raise the stakes. Remember, start with smaller issues and gradually move on to bigger ones.

But never forget, as long as we are on this side of Glory, we're subject to missing God. Even today, after years of walking in the Spirit and after remarkable success at it, I am still very cautious. Interestingly, sometimes I hear from God loud and clear, and sometimes I wonder if I am hearing from Him at all. Here's some good advice: You need to establish your own working relationship with God.

To build and maintain a good relationship with your spouse, your child, or a friend, you have to continually work at it—making an effort every day to spend quality time with them, talk to them, and listen to what they have to say. It's the same with the Holy Spirit. I believe everyone should have a personal working relationship with Him; after all, He's our Helper.

And I will pray the Father, and he shall give you another
Comforter [Helper⁴], that he may abide with you for ever;
Even the Spirit of truth; whom the world cannot receive,
because it seeth him not, neither knoweth him: but ye know
him; for he dwelleth with you, and shall be in you.

JOHN 14:16,17

I established my working arrangement with the Holy Spirit long ago, and He's always honored it. I said to Him, "You know me, Lord. I can be dense at times. If You want me to do something, You have to make it plain to me. I'm not rebellious; I just don't want to miss the mark. You're intelligent and I'm intelligent; You can communicate to me in a way I understand. I can't step out if I'm unsure. When I'm sure I'll step out and obey You." I can honestly say that when I've been consistent and paid attention to His leading, He's made things plain for me.

God is consistent. We need to be consistent. Don't be hot one day and cold the next. Be consistent, and pay attention.

This is powerful information, isn't it? In the next chapter, I'll prove to you that this isn't something I merely made up. *The easy way to walk in the Spirit* is biblical.

5

tried-and-true witness

You may be wondering, "Is there anywhere in the Bible where others operated this way of being led by the Spirit?" I'm glad you asked.

But first, let me ask you a question. In your opinion, next to Jesus, who is the most important man in the New Testament? If you said the apostle Paul, then you and I are in agreement.

Paul was God's vessel, chosen to spread Christianity to the world beyond Israel. He wrote the majority of the New Testament, including the powerful revelation of "Christ in you, the hope of glory" (Col. 1:27). In telling us what happened from the cross to the throne, he taught us about the substitutionary work of Christ, the Atonement, the gifts of the Spirit, and much more.

How did this great apostle operate? How did the Spirit lead him?

Read the next passage carefully. You may be surprised to discover that Paul used the easy way to be led by the Spirit at least once.

> *Now when they [Paul and Silas] had gone throughout Phrygia and the region of Galatia, and were forbidden of the Holy Ghost to preach the word in Asia,*
>
> *After they were come to Mysia, they assayed to go into Bithynia: but the Spirit suffered them not.*
>
> *And they passing by Mysia came down to Troas.*
>
> *And a vision appeared to Paul in the night; There stood a man of Macedonia, and prayed him, saying, Come over into Macedonia, and help us.*
>
> *And after he had seen the vision, immediately we endeavored to go into Macedonia, assuredly gathering that the Lord had called us for to preach the gospel unto them.*
>
> *Therefore loosing from Troas, we came with a straight course to Samothracia, and the next day to Neapolis.*
>
> ACTS 16:6-11

Notice that Paul and Silas went through the region of Phrygia and Galatia, but they got a check in their spirit when they attempted to go to Asia. The Bible says that the Holy Spirit forbade them to preach there. *Forbidden* is another word for *no*. They *assayed* (tested, attempted, endeavored)[1] to go to Bithinia, "but the Spirit suffered them not." That's also another way of saying *no*. Finally, they got a *yes*, "Come over into Macedonia...."

This was how the great apostle Paul operated. Doesn't that seem like trial and error? Had we been in Silas's shoes we might have wondered about Paul: *It seems, he knows where not to go more than he knows where to go!*

Surely the great apostle Paul could have prayed and received his entire itinerary from God. Isn't that the way we want to do it? We want to know the whole picture at the very beginning. Certainly Paul prayed, but he still got it a little at a time as he moved forward, step-by-step—and so do we.

God usually leads us as we move. Remember, Jesus said, "Go ye..." (Mark 16:15). Have you noticed that God is always on the move? Just as you can't steer a parked car, and you can't sail an anchored boat, God can't steer us unless we're moving forward.

And thine ears shall hear a word behind thee, saying, This is the way, walk ye in it, when ye turn to the right hand, and when ye turn to the left.

ISAIAH 30:21

This Scripture reminds me of the old omni-directional navigation system pilots used in the early days of radio navigation. If they strayed left of their course, they heard a distinctive beep and corrected back to the right. Or, if they heard the distinctive tone, indicating they had strayed to the right of their course, they would correct to the left.

Navigating an airplane is much like walking with God. In reality, a true course for an airplane exists only on paper, as a line drawn between two points. Pilots fly adjusted headings. They adjust for wind, magnetic deviation, airplane trim, and pilot error. Walking in the Spirit requires the same diligence. We must constantly monitor our heading and correct for errors. Skilled pilots make many small corrections. Unskilled pilots wait until they're in trouble; then they make violent corrections.

How did Paul navigate the will of God? Each time he got a check in his spirit, he corrected his heading, until he got the witness of the Spirit indicating that he was on target.

If *the easy way to walk in the Spirit* worked for Paul, it can work for you and me.

walking step-by-step

Before we look to the Old Testament for an example of someone else using this method, here's another quiz. In your opinion, which Old Testament prophet had the most important historical decision to make?

If you answered Samuel, you and I are in agreement. Why do I think it was Samuel? He was the one who discovered and anointed God's choice for king of Israel!

Jesus, the Messiah, was of the lineage of David, and He sits upon the throne of David. (Luke 1:32.) Had Samuel missed the mark and chosen the wrong man, the messianic lineage would have been altered (and that's unthinkable). Where would we be without David? No Psalms, no Solomon, no Joseph, no Mary, no Jesus, no salvation, no hope. Thank God Samuel knew how to be led by the Spirit!

How did Samuel discover God's man for the throne? To begin with, Samuel had a *general* direction. God told him to go to the house of Jesse, "...for I have provided me a king among his sons" (1 Sam. 16:1). But to choose the wrong son would be a disaster. Here's how Samuel made his decision.

And it came to pass, when they were come, that he looked on Eliab, and said, Surely the Lord's anointed is before him.

But the Lord said unto Samuel, Look not on his countenance, or on the height of his stature; because I have refused him: for the Lord seeth not as man seeth; for man looketh on the outward appearance, but the Lord looketh on the heart.

Then Jesse called Abinadab, and made him pass before Samuel. And he said, Neither hath the Lord chosen this.

Then Jesse made Shammah to pass by. And he said, Neither hath the Lord chosen this.

Again, Jesse made seven of his sons to pass before Samuel. And Samuel said unto Jesse, The Lord hath not chosen these.

And Samuel said unto Jesse, Are here all thy children? And he said, There remaineth yet the youngest, and, behold, he

keepeth the sheep. And Samuel said unto Jesse, Send and fetch
him: for we will not sit down till he come hither.

And he sent, and brought him in. Now he was ruddy, and
withal of a beautiful countenance, and goodly to look to. And
the Lord said, Arise, anoint him: for this is he.

1 SAMUEL 16:6-12

As Jesse's sons came before the prophet, Samuel inquired
of the Lord. He looked at each of the first three and asked,
"God, is it Eliab?" [No] "God, is it Abinadab?" [No] "God, is
it Shammah?" [No]. Notice that three times Samuel got a
check in his spirit.

Four more of Jesse's sons passed before Samuel, and
Samuel got four more checks in his spirit.

Do you remember what I said earlier about asking a *differ-*
ent question? Samuel probably thought awhile, and then he
asked, "Are here all thy children?"

Jesse answered, "There remaineth yet the youngest, and,
behold, he keepeth the sheep," to which Samuel immediately
said, "Send and fetch him." But not until Samuel stood
before David did Samuel receive his witness of the Spirit that
David was the one: "And the Lord said, Arise, anoint him: for
this is he."

Did you see how that worked? Just as I said, by the witness
of the Spirit.

Wouldn't you think a great prophet like Samuel could stay at home and get David's resume from God? That's what we would like to do—get the answer, the plan, right away from the Master Planner. But the way to walk in the Spirit is by, well, *walking* step-by-step.

making the right decision

I want to point out a few things about how Samuel made the most important decision of his life. One, he went forward one step at a time. Two, all his decisions could have been answered by a simple yes or no (in fact, basically he received seven *no's* and one *yes*). Four, he responded to the witness of the Spirit, immediately. Yes, I skipped number *three* because I want to talk about it in detail.

The third thing Samuel did was, he stood face-to-face with his situation before he got his answer. This is an important point.

Often, you will get the witness of the Spirit at the very point of decision. For example, you may not know where you're supposed to work until the *last* interview. You may not know which new house you're supposed to buy until you walk through it, or even at the closing. When you stand face-to-face with your situation, examine your spirit; that may be when you get a witness of the Spirit (or a check in your spirit) about what to do or which way to go.

You must be willing to instantly obey the Holy Spirit. Even if you're about to sign that big contract, should you get a check in your spirit, back out of the deal. It may be embarrassing, but it will save you a hundred miles of bad road.

Think back. Remember that Paul and Silas, "...assayed to go into Bithynia" (Acts 16:7). We saw earlier that the word *assayed* means to attempt, test, endeavor[1]. They *endeavored* to go, or they *attempted* to go, but they were stopped by the witness of the Spirit before they got there. My advice is, go slow if you don't know; you can go fast once you have the witness.

timing is everything

Returning to Paul's experience, we can observe another nuance of the Spirit. With God, no means no, but it doesn't necessarily mean *never*. You will discover that with God, timing is everything.

On his first missionary trip, Paul was forbidden by God to preach in Asia Minor. However, eventually God allowed him to go to Asia, where he had his earth-shaking revival at Ephesus.

Sometimes God redirects us to adjust our timing. He slows us down when we are moving too fast. He speeds us up when we're moving too slow. Once, I had the Spirit tell me, "Don't think about leaving San Francisco." Then, in another season, He redirected me to Mexico. It's all about timing.

The easy way to walk in the Spirit will serve you anywhere, anytime. It's the default method that works when God isn't appearing in burning bushes (Ex. 3:3,4) or thundering from heaven. (Job 40:9.) It's a process of simplification. We begin with the general and work down to the specific.

Think again about the apostle Paul and the prophet Samuel. They didn't hit the bull's-eye on the first try. If they had big egos, they would have been embarrassed. I mean, prophets are supposed to impress us with their accuracy, right?

If Samuel's true intent for visiting Bethlehem had been known, I don't think he would have impressed anyone at first. "Oh, it's not Eliab? Excuse me, sorry. Oh, it's not Abinadab? Sorry! Uh, I don't know what's happening. Not Shammah? Oh my! I'm having a bad day." Then an hour later, "Do you have another boy?"

I wonder what Silas thought about traveling with Paul.

"Where are we going, Paul?" "Asia...Uh, sorry Silas, it's not Asia, not now. Maybe Mysia...No, sorry, not Mysia, either. Bythinia...Ha! Silas, would you believe I got another check in my spirit? It's Macedonia, I'm sure of it. Yes, I had a dream..."

I wonder if Silas thought, *Maybe, I should have gone with Barnabus.*

It may look hit-and-miss, but it's not. It's a walk of faith. Most people never attempt to walk in the Spirit because they are afraid of missing it. I think that's pride in some cases. Besides, you haven't missed it until you quit.

Learning to walk in the Spirit is like learning to walk. Toddlers fall, but we don't say, "You dumb baby, you may as well quit!" No, before long they're running, skipping, and jumping.

On the other hand, we would be alarmed if they didn't attempt to walk. We would take them to the doctor to have them checked out. "Doctor, is something wrong with Junior? He doesn't walk."

"Hum, how old is Junior?"

"Just twenty years old."

I'm concerned about *adult* Christians who have never learned to walk in the Spirit. That's arrested development of the worst kind. At least try to crawl. Don't sit there like a blob of quivering Jell-O.

follow the witness

I remember a couple of incidents that happened to me many years ago, when the Holy Spirit first started developing this in me.

Once, I was sitting on the platform on Sunday morning, while our senior pastor was preaching. Suddenly the Holy Spirit said to me, "There's a woman here with a hernia. I want you to call her out of the congregation and pray for her."

My initial response was, "No, Lord, I'm not going to do that. I don't mean to tell You Your business, but, as far as I know, hernias happen to men, in the groin area, not women." But again the Lord said, "There's a woman here with a hernia; call her out."

Still I protested, "No, I don't think that's a good idea. You want me to say, 'There's a woman here with a hernia,' and everyone's going to laugh me to scorn, because women don't have hernias." (I didn't know any better at the time.)

The Lord said, "Nothing bad is going to happen. Call her out."

I started negotiating. "Lord, do I have to say, 'There's a *woman* here?' Can't I say, 'There's *someone* here with a hernia?'"

"Okay," He said. "Do it your way."

Of course, all this happened in my heart, not aloud. Outwardly, I was sitting there looking as intelligent as I could.

Soon the pastor turned to me and said, "Brother Huggins, I think you have something from the Lord. Come up here and obey God." So I took the microphone and said, "As a matter of fact I do. There's someone here today with a hernia. God wants to heal you. If you have a hernia, come up and I'll pray for you."

As God is my witness, about four men came up. I thought, *See, God, what did I tell You—all men.*

I prayed, and I could see that the power of God came on them. Soon they returned to their seats, healed and blessed, but I didn't feel released by God from praying for someone with a hernia. So I announced, "There's still someone who didn't respond. Come up here, and I'll pray for you, too."

Three more men came, and the same blessing came on them, but I wasn't done. When I tried to quit, the Spirit checked me.

"There's still someone here with a hernia," I said, and when I announced that, two more men came up. (I've never seen so many hernias in one place.)

Finally, I said, "Folks, in my spirit, I know there's at least one more person here with a hernia."

Suddenly a lady stood to her feet! I pointed at her and declared, "Lady, it's you! The Lord wanted to heal you all the time."

She came and stood before me, with her arms raised, and whispered, "How did you know it was me?" I whispered back, "Ask me after church."

Later, I confessed to her how I had doubted that women had hernias, and she said, "Oh yes, it's a hiatal hernia, and it's in the diaphragm area of my body."

Well, I learned two things that day. One, God is smarter than I am. Two, you have to keep following the witness of the Spirit, one step at a time.

another learning experience

There was another incident a few months later. We had moved our congregation to a larger facility. During the second service one Sunday I was sitting on the platform, in my usual place. While the pastor was up preaching, the Lord said to me, "There's a woman here with symptoms of cancer, but it isn't cancer. Call her out and minister to her." So I said, "Okay, Lord, when I have the opportunity, I will."

While I was sitting there, I decided to try and figure out who this woman was. There were about seven hundred adults in the ten o'clock service. After I eliminated all the men, I had narrowed my search to about three hundred and fifty.

I couldn't get out of my seat and go stand before each woman (as Samuel had done with Jesse's sons). So, I gazed at each woman from where I sat. I searched section by section, row by row, and woman by woman, asking, "Lord, is it her? [No] Is it her? [No] Is it her? [No]."

In a few minutes' time, I had looked at each woman and gotten about three hundred and fifty checks in my spirit. I was puzzled. Then I thought of another question. "Lord, is there a woman in this sanctuary that I can't see from where I'm sitting?" We had a few bad seats.

Then I began leaning out of my seat and looking behind the posts near the back of the room, and there she was; I had the witness of the Spirit. I knew her name, but she didn't look like she was having symptoms; she looked healthy. *Surely it's not her,* I thought. But the witness of the Spirit told me it was.

A few minutes later the pastor said, "Brother Huggins, I think you have something from the Spirit. Come up here and obey God." So I walked up to the pulpit and said, "There's a woman here with symptoms of cancer. Come up here, and I'll pray for you."

Who do you think jumped up and ran to the altar? You're exactly right, the lady behind the post. Out of seven hundred people I had picked the right person by the witness of the Spirit. Praise God!

That was a long time ago, and I was timid back then. If I had known then what I know now, I would have pointed my finger at her, and with Old Testament flair, called her by name and thundered, "Sister, the devil has lied to you. He told you that you have the symptoms of cancer. But God has told me you do not. Be free, in Jesus' name!"

Wow, wouldn't that have been great? Well, she was set free anyway. It really blessed her, and it glorified Jesus. But for me it was a learning experience—it helped me to learn how to ask the Holy Spirit simple questions that He can answer with a simple *yes* or *no*. Of course, when I ask Him something, I don't listen for an audible voice, but for the witness of the Spirit.

service, edification, and blessings

As I've been writing this book, sometimes I've felt as though I'm giving away trade secrets. But this information is so powerful, it can revolutionize your life. There's no way you can place a value upon what you've just learned.

So I hope that all this is clear to you. If you understand what I'm saying, you can learn the easy way to be led by the Spirit. Again, I'm not talking about an audible sound. I'm talking about a spiritual truth.

I must caution you one more time. Don't abuse this gift. Don't play games with it, please. God hasn't given us this gift for self-aggrandizement, but for service unto Him and the edification of others.

But ye shall receive power, after that the Holy Ghost is come upon you: and ye shall be witnesses unto me both in Jerusalem, and in all Judaea, and in Samaria, and unto the uttermost part of the earth.

ACTS 1:8

The power of the Holy Spirit enables us to give strong testimony that Jesus Christ is Lord and the Word of God works. But you will also be blessed in deed, now that you know *the easy way to walk in the Spirit.*

There are deeper and higher experiences awaiting you as you grow in the knowledge of God. Walking in the Spirit is just one of the countless blessings that are available to those "who hunger and thirst after righteousness [spiritual blessings[2]]" (Matt. 5:6). May God's richest and best be yours, always.

review

Let's review a few highlights of what we've learned:

Be a lover of the truth.

Stay in the Word of God.

Pray in the Spirit overtime.

Check your motives.

Ask simple yes or no questions.

Pay attention to the witness of the Spirit.

Be willing to rephrase your questions.

Take it step-by-step.

Mend and adjust as necessary.

Glorify God, not yourself.

Don't forget these additional points:

Give yourself time to grow; you have to walk before you run.

You may have to stand face-to-face with your situation before you get your answer.

With God, no means *no;* but occasionally it might mean *not now.*

Develop your personal working relationship with the Holy Spirit.

Go slow if you don't know; you can go fast once you have the witness.

more benefits of walking in the spirit

In the light of what you have just learned, read the following passage from the letter to the Romans, in Romans chapter 8. I believe that it will bless you, as you discover even more benefits of walking in the Spirit.

Romans 8:1-16 (KJV)

1 There is therefore now no condemnation to them which are in Christ Jesus, who walk not after the flesh, but after the Spirit.

2 For the law of the Spirit of life in Christ Jesus hath made me free from the law of sin and death.

3 For what the law could not do, in that it was weak through the flesh, God sending his own Son in the likeness of sinful flesh, and for sin, condemned sin in the flesh:

4 That the righteousness of the law might be fulfilled in us, who walk not after the flesh, but after the Spirit.

5 For they that are after the flesh do mind the things of the flesh; but they that are after the Spirit the things of the Spirit.

6 For to be carnally minded is death; but to be spiritually minded is life and peace.

7 Because the carnal mind is enmity against God: for it is not subject to the law of God, neither indeed can be.

8 So then they that are in the flesh cannot please God.

9 But ye are not in the flesh, but in the Spirit, if so be that the Spirit of God dwell in you. Now if any man have not the Spirit of Christ, he is none of his.

10 And if Christ be in you, the body is dead because of sin; but the Spirit is life because of righteousness.

11 But if the Spirit of him that raised up Jesus from the dead dwell in you, he that raised up Christ from the dead shall also quicken your mortal bodies by his Spirit that dwelleth in you.

12 Therefore, brethren, we are debtors, not to the flesh, to live after the flesh.

13 For if ye live after the flesh, ye shall die: but if ye through the Spirit do mortify the deeds of the body, ye shall live.

14 For as many as are led by the Spirit of God, they are the sons of God.

15 For ye have not received the spirit of bondage again to fear; but ye have received the Spirit of adoption, whereby we cry, Abba, Father.

16 The Spirit itself beareth witness with our spirit, that we are the children of God:

endnotes

Introduction

[1] Praying in the Spirit refers to a heavenly prayer language available to all who believe, which is inspired by the Holy Spirit.

[2] "[diverse] kinds of tongues—the power of speaking...a spiritual language unknown to man...(1 Cor. 14:2-12)... interpretation of [diverse] tongues—(1 Cor. 14:13,26,27)."

[3] Robert Jamieson, A.R. Fausset, and David Brown, *Commentary Critical and Explanatory on the Whole Bible,* "The First Epistle of Paul the Apostle to the Corinthians" (Blue Letter Bible, 2000, 2004), s.v. "1 Corinthians 14:12," available from <http://www.blueletter-bible.org/Comm/jfb/1Cr/1Cr012.html>.

Chapter 2

[1] *Merriam-Webster Collegiate Dictionary,* Tenth Edition (Springfield, Massachusetts: 2000), s.v. "relativism."

[2] Ibid., s.v. "republic."

[3] Argentine doctor who left his profession to become a revolutionary leader (first in Cuba) in the 1950s and 1960s.

[4] Thayer and Smith, *The KJV New Testament Greek Lexicon,* "Greek Lexicon entry for Poneria," s.v. "iniquity," Acts 3:26, available from <http://www.biblestudytools.net/Lexicons/Greek/grk.cgi?number=4 189&version=kjv>.

Chapter 3

1. Based on a definition from *The KJV New Testament Greek Lexicon,* "Greek Lexicon entry for Summartureo," S.V. "witness," Romans 9:1, available from <http://www.biblestudytools.net/Lexicons/Greek/grk.cgi?number=4828&version=kjv>.

2. *New Exhaustive Strong's Numbers and Concordance with Expanded Greek-Hebrew Dictionary* (Electronic Database: Biblesoft and International Bible Translators, Inc., 1994).

3. Based upon a definition from Thayer and Smith, "Greek Lexicon entry for Martureo," S.V. "bear witness," John 5:31, available from <http://www.biblestudytools.net/Lexicons/Greek/grk.cgi?number=3 140&version=kjv>.

4. Matthew Henry, *Matthew Henry Complete Commentary on the Whole Bible,* "Commentary on John 5," S.V. "31-37," available from <http://bible.crosswalk.com/Commentaries/MatthewHenryComple te/mhc-com.cgi?book=joh&chapter=005>.

5. "...It should not seem strange to us that false teachers set themselves up in the church: it was so in the apostles' times; ...He [Paul] gives a test whereby the disciples may try these pretending spirits...they were to be tried by their doctrine; and the test...must be this: *Hereby know you the Spirit of God, Every spirit that confesseth that Jesus Christ has come in the flesh (or that confesseth Jesus Christ that came in the flesh), is of God....*" Ibid., S.V. "1 John 4:1-3," available from <http://www.blueletterbible.org/Comm/mhc/1Jo/1Jo004.html>.

6. Thayer and Smith, "Greek Lexicon entry for Dokimazo," S.V. "try," 1 John 4:1, available from <http://www.biblestudytools.net/Lexicons/Greek/grk.cgi?number=1381&version=kjv>.

7. W. E. Vine, *Vine's Expository Dictionary of New Testament Words Words* (McLean, Virginia: MacDonald Publishing Company), p. 45, S.V. "AGREE, AGREEMENT."

[8] Based on a definition from Thayer and Smith, "Greek Lexicon entry for Martureo," S.V. "bear record," 1 John 5:7, available from <http://www.biblestudytools.net/Lexicons/Greek/grk.cgi?number=3 140&version=kjv>.

[1] We become a new creation when we invite Jesus into our heart and become born again. If you have never done that and would like to, there's a prayer you can pray at the end of this book.

Chapter 4

[1] Strong's, entry #205, S.V. "iniquity," Psalm 66:18.

[2] Thayer and Smith, "Greek Lexicon entry for Metanoeo," S.V. "repent," available from <http://www.biblestudytools.net/Lexicons/Greek/grk.cgi?number=3340&version=kjv>.

[3] Albert Barnes, Barnes' Notes on the New Testament, "Commentary on James 4," S.V. "James 4:3," available from <http://www.studylight.org/com/bnn/view.cgi?book=jas&chapter=004>.

[4] Thayer and Smith, "Greek Lexicon entry for Parakletos," S.V. "Comforter," John 14:16, available from <http://www.biblestudytools.net/Lexicons/Greek/grk.cgi?number=3875&version=kjv>.

Chapter 5

[1] Based upon a definition from Strong's, entry #3985, S.V. "assay," Acts. 16:7.

[2] Matthew Henry, "Commentary on Matthew 5," S.V. "Matthew 5:3-12, IV," available from <http://bible.crosswalk.com/Commentaries/MatthewHenryComplete/mhc-com.cgi?book=mt&chapter=005>.

prayer of salvation

God loves you—no matter who you are, no matter what your past. God loves you so much that He gave His one and only begotten Son for you. The Bible tells us that "...whoever believes in him shall not perish but have eternal life" (John 3:16 NIV). Jesus laid down His life and rose again so that we could spend eternity with Him in heaven and experience His absolute best on earth. If you would like to receive Jesus into your life, say the following prayer out loud and mean it from your heart.

Heavenly Father, I come to You admitting that I am a sinner. Right now, I choose to turn away from sin, and I ask You to cleanse me of all unrighteousness. I believe that Your Son, Jesus, died on the cross to take away my sins. I also believe that He rose again from the dead so that I might be forgiven of my sins and made righteous through faith in Him. I call upon the name of Jesus Christ to be the Savior and Lord of my life. Jesus, I choose to follow You and ask that You fill me with the power of the Holy Spirit. I declare that right now I am a child of God. I am free from sin and full of the righteousness of God. I am saved in Jesus' name. Amen.

If you prayed this prayer to receive Jesus Christ as your Savior for the first time, please contact us on the Web at **www.harrisonhouse.com** to receive a free book.

Or you may write to us at
Harrison House
P.O. Box 35035
Tulsa, Oklahoma 74153

about the author

Rev. Larry Huggins, author and missionary statesman, has surrounded the world with his faith and love since the Lord appeared to him and called him into His service as a young man. Countless numbers of people have attended his miracle crusades and teaching seminars overseas and across the nation. Larry first began preaching in Arkansas mountain "wood-stove" community churches as he calls them. Today, Ambassador Huggins' calling has taken him many times around the world to fifty-nine nations.

Rev. Huggins' powerful ministry is a balance of the Word and the Spirit. Working with him, Jesus confirms the Word with signs following.

Formerly called "Ambassador International Ministries," Larry's ministry is now called "The Commonwealth of Christ." His beautiful wife, Loretta, works beside him in the ministry, and is a popular conference speaker in her own right. They have four sons, one grandson, and one granddaughter.

Rev. Huggins is a popular convention and seminar speaker, well known for his prophetic and inspirational ministry.

other books by larry huggins

The Blood Speaks

The Cup of Blessing

To contact Larry Huggins,
please write to:

Larry Huggins
The Commonwealth of Christ
AKA Ambassador International Ministries, Inc.
P.O. Box 140645
Austin, TX 78714
Or call 1-888-YES-LIFE

E-mail Address: Ambassador@kingsembassy.com
http://kingsembassy.com

*Please include your prayer requests
and praise reports when you write.*

www.harrisonhouse.com
Fast. Easy. Convenient!

◆ New Book Information
◆ Look Inside the Book
◆ Press Releases
◆ Bestsellers

◆ Free E-News
◆ Author Biographies
◆ Upcoming Books
◆ Share Your Testimony

For the latest in book news and author information, please visit us on the Web at www.harrisonhouse.com. Get up-to-date pictures and details on all our powerful and life-changing products. Sign up for our e-mail newsletter, *Friends of the House,* and receive free monthly information on our authors and products including testimonials, author announcements, and more!

Harrison House—
Books That Bring Hope, Books That Bring Change

the harrison house vision

Proclaiming the truth and the power

Of the Gospel of Jesus Christ

With excellence;

Challenging Christians to

Live victoriously,

Grow spiritually,

Know God intimately.